Dan M. Pelletier
Illustrated by Callie L. French

LA SANTA MUERTE

LENORMAND

4880 Lower Valley Road, Atglen, PA 19310

Copyright © 2022 by Dan M. Pelletier and Callie L. French

Library of Congress Control Number: 2021942592

All rights reserved. No part of this work may be reproduced or used in any form or by any means—graphic, electronic, or mechanical, including photocopying or information storage and retrieval systems—without written permission from the publisher.

"Red Feather Mind Body Spirit" logo is a trademark of Schiffer Publishing, Ltd. | "Red Feather Mind Body Spirit Feather" logo is a registered trademark of Schiffer Publishing, Ltd.

Designed by Brenda McCallum
Type set in Optima/Phenomenologist
ISBN: 978-0-7643-6377-1
Printed in India

Published by REDFeather Mind, Body, Spirit
An imprint of Schiffer Publishing, Ltd.
4880 Lower Valley Road
Atglen, PA 19310
Phone: (610) 593-1777; Fax: (610) 593-2002
Email: Info@redfeathermbs.com
Web: www.redfeathermbs.com

PREFACE

La Santa Muerte (Spanish for "Our Lady of the Holy Death"), who appears as a skeletal figure, usually in flowing gowns, can be a prickly subject. I have heard vehement accusations of "cultural appropriation" from Anglos, leveled at other Anglos and non–Roman Catholics who venerate what some consider a "Mexican Catholic folk goddess of death." Others, who may suffer from thanatophobia, also beat the drum of misunderstanding and prejudice when it comes to discussing *la Santísima Muerte* ("the Most Holy Death"). So, discussing historical facts is important to prevent disagreements.

There are a few competing origin theories of Santa Muerte, and no universal origin theory. One theory has her evolving from the Aztec deity Mictēcacihuātl (Goddess of Death), and since Aztec culture was destroyed by the Spanish colonials and the Inquisition of their church, her worship was hidden, and aspects of the Roman Catholicism and the colonial "archetypes" were adopted.

There are references to La Santísima Muerte in 1793, and then she vanishes only to reappear in the 1940s, when she resurfaces primarily as a "folk saint" focused mainly on love.

The second theory traces the lineage of La Flaca ("the Skinny Girl") from the Moirai of Greece (Atopos) to Rome, in the form of the Parcae (the Fates), and Parca Morta (Fate of Death). Parca Morta was a skeletal figure outfitted with reaping implements, an hourglass, and scales. La Parca (the Parched One), a female Grim Reaper, dates to the plague years. Veneration of La Parca likely was imported by Hernán Cortés and the early colonists to Mesoamerica, along with the practices of the Catholic Church. Cultural evolution may have occurred (specifically regarding Mictēcacihuātl).

La Flaca would have been easily recognizable by and acceptable to the natives, since their heritage had been overthrown; La Parca and Mictēcacihuātl became as one, not only in Mexico but also extending into what is now considered the southwestern United States. I believe both accounts are correct.

Regardless of the origins, Señora de la

Noche ("Our Lady of the Night") migrated across the borders of Mexico many decades ago. She traveled to the islands, around the Gulf states, and up both coasts of Norteamérica. Her following is now global. With her growth, there are necessary differences in devotional practices due to cultural, linguistic, and geographical differences.

Many consider Señora de la Noche to be evil, a death goddess. That is not the entire truth; although she is death, she directs us to celebrate life. *Santísima Muerte* is associated with love, healing, protection, financial well-being, justice, and assurance of a path to the afterlife.

Señora de las Sombras ("Lady of the Shadows," "Shadow Lady") is often invoked by those endangered by working at night or living on the margins of society: taxi drivers, bartenders, night cleaning staff, after-hours maintenance persons, police, soldiers, exotic dancers, waiters and waitresses, prostitutes, street vendors, vendors of counterfeit merchandise, street people, single mothers, pickpockets, petty drug traffickers, members of the LGBTQ+ community, gang members, and the mentally ill. La Santa Muerte has protected people the world over from acts of hostility, brutality, and illness.

The media has incorrectly portrayed her as principally a "narco-saint," but she provides aid for all. "La Santa Muerte no discrimina"; everyone—rich, poor, and somewhere in between—will eventually get to dance with her, and in the meantime, she listens to the prayers of all. She does not judge. She is a true neutral figure.

Even though her roots appear to stem from Roman Catholicism, La Santa Muerte does not demand exclusive devotion. Many followers also practice other religions, such as Catholicism, Protestantism, Judaism, Wicca, Santeria, and other "spiritual" practices.

Therefore, in this guidebook, we shall not address how to practice your devotions to La Santa Muerte. Our focus instead shall be on using this particular deck of Lenormand cards as an oracular system. How you incorporate her into your divinatory practice is your business.

Further, there will be users who may object

that my approach is not the French approach but aligns with the eastern European approach. There are specific reasons for this, related to the Skeleton Saint (think Cinco de Mayo).

To summarize, if you are looking for a book to tell you how to become a devotee of La Santa Muerte, you will not find that information here. It is not our place to tell you how to practice your spiritual life.

If you are looking for a book that will reveal all the secrets of the Lenormand divination system, you will not find it here; we choose to reveal only a few crucial nuggets. A Grand Tableau? There are many other fine books by great authors who can guide you through your first attempts at learning to read a Grande Tableau.

This booklet is written with the assumption you are already a follower of La Santa Muerte (or soon will be), and if this is your first Lenormand deck, we've included everything to get you on the road to reading Lenormand well.

La Santa Muerte aids her devotees before her harvest, in areas of love, health, abundance, substance abuse, blockages, and legal troubles.

A final word needs to be shared here. She answers prayers that other saints often will not. The creators and the publishers shall not be held responsible for unintended consequences of devotional requests.

A BRIEF HISTORY OF LENORMAND CARDS

The modern deck of Lenormand cards began as what is called a race game (a race game is where one tries to get their pieces to the "end" before others; Snakes and Ladders, Parcheesi, and Backgammon are examples), this version being like a board game without a board. The cards (called sheets in the instructions) were laid out in numerical order (using the numbers on each card), and then each player moved tokens from sheet to sheet as determined by a roll of the dice.

It was first published as Das Spiel der Hofnung (the Game of Hope) in Nuremberg, Germany, by Johann Kaspar Hechtel in 1799 (published by Gustav Philipp Jakob Bieling Publishing House). The deck used 36 cards and, in addition to the symbols, contained playing-card images using both German (Ansbach pattern) suits, and one using French (Bavarian Paris pattern) suits, so that in addition to playing "the Game of Hope," any number of other card games could be played. Games using 36 and 32 cards were quite common (and still are). They were published and sold as parlor games.

It was not until around 50 years later that the idea of a parlor game using dice was dropped, and the cards became known as Lenormand cards, in a marketing ploy.

Marie Anne Adelaide Lenormand (1772–1843) was a fortune-teller who used regular playing cards as an oracular tool (cartomancy). She was an excellent example of brilliant self-marketing, and she created a personal brand during the Napoleonic era in France.

She stated that she had read for Empress Josephine, Robespierre, Marat, Saint-Just, and Alexander I of Russia, and other personages of the higher echelons. Her claims are accounted for by her own hand in her writings. She published 15 known books and monographs during her life.

We also know she was arrested numerous times for fraud.

It has been documented that she preferred to read with a 32-card deck, and occasionally with what now would be called Tarot de Marseille (and not an Etteilla deck).

Around 1850 (Mlle. Lenormand was dead by then), the first 36-card "Petit Lenormand" decks began to appear. That they were 36-card decks as opposed to 32-card decks points to German origin (32-card games were popular in France, whereas 36-card games were popular in Germany), and the use of the name "Lenormand" indicates brilliant marketing, turning a race game into a fortune-telling game.

PRACTICALITY OF THE LENORMAND SYSTEM

The Lenormand system came out of a time (1799) when literacy rates were rather low. There were not books written on "how to read" the cards. But everybody knew what a scythe was and what it was for. They knew what a coffin and an anchor were and what their purpose was. What is referred to as the Lenormand system is built around vocabulary. The words you speak. The words you use.

For each card, we want you to think of it in a couple of ways. First, what is it? What does it do? That's it. A tree. It grows. It gives shade. Growth is healthy. So, a tree represents growth, health, and a "long time" (trees grow slowly).

Then we think of it as a modifier, as verbs and adjectives. The tree does not move and really cannot move. It has roots and may appear to be stuck. And if it is too close to the house, it is not good. Paired with mice? Doubly not good.

That is really the secret. "What is it?" and "What does it do?" The symbols are essentially representative of nouns and modifiers. When we get to the descriptions of the cards, the listed words are not really meanings but are examples of nouns and modifiers that may be used in conjunction with the cards in a spread.

There are a few additional items to add to the Lenormand system of card reading.

Each card has the symbol (and the name) of a "traditional playing card" associated with that symbol, and a number designating where its place is in the ordinal sequence of the cards.

I would like to also address the playing-card insets. Why are they there? What do they mean? We know from the original instructions of Das Spiel der Hofnung that the game was played by laying the cards out in numerical order. We are not told about the insets.

We also know that the original deck contained two insets, one using German suits and one using French suits.

The original instructions state, "In order to play any conceivable card game played with ordinary German and French playing cards with these 36 figure cards for further entertainment, the German and French card pictures have been included at the top of the cards. It is only sometimes necessary to leave the sixes and the sevens out of the game. Also, this makes it very easy to learn to compare the German and French cards."

The cards were originally published for entertainment purposes. Were the insets originally used for cartomantic purposes? Probably not.

At the end of the instructions for the Game of Hope, it states: "With these same cards, it is also possible to play an entertaining game of oracles by shuffling the 36 cards and then letting the person, for whom the oracle is meant, cut the cards, then laying out the cards in five rows with four rows of eight cards each, and the fifth row with the remaining four cards. If the person querying is a woman, one starts from sheet 29, spinning a jocular tale from the cards nearby around the figures on display. If it is for a man, the tale is started from sheet 28 and again makes use of the cards surrounding this one. This will bring much entertainment to any merry company." That was the entirety of how to tell fortunes with the cards. Everything else came later.

Here it is beneficial to discuss the suits of the insets, since they have a direct impact on the final card interpretation.

These are the German suits as compared with the French suits:

acorns = clubs
hearts = hearts

bells = diamonds
leaves = spades

In the German system, spades are always good and positive. Leaves show growth.

Acorns are horrid and bitter, edible only by those too poor to feed themselves, or animals.

Hearts are emotions. Usually they are good, but sometimes . . .

Bells are alarms, things to take note of. Essentially neutral.

The numerical values of the insets (which generally are considered to run from six to ace) have been "decoded" by some authors. As of 2005, I have found over 12 different cartomantic systems for 52-card oracle systems, and here I find nothing uniform. The Pythagorean numerology does not correlate with the card symbols.

I do, however, use the suits, relying on them heavily: how they account themselves in number and arrangement.

I also find the gender of the courts to add flavor.

READING WITH THE LENORMAND SYSTEM

Learning to read with two cards is the easiest and best learning method.

It begins with a simple question. The question provides the context for the card meanings. It must be simple and not multi-pronged.

Third-party questions—health, finance, and some legal—and questions relating to gambling outcomes usually produce confusing and erroneous answers. There are too many variables. Further, Nuestra Señora de la Santa Muerte usually will not provide favorable answers for trivial matters. Keep your question personal and simple.

Most readers will use the first card as a noun. The next card is a modifier; it modifies the first card. You may reverse this if the context of the question dictates it.

One begins by creating a two-card sentence. Many will complain that you need more cards. Eventually you will graduate to three, but everyone should begin with two.

You can do a lot with two cards; there's a story (actually a myth) that Ernest Hemingway once wrote a story using only six words: "For sale. Baby shoes. Never worn."

And that is how we begin.

Later, you can begin to use three or five cards.

In larger layouts (a 3×3 or a Grand Tableau), a significator card may be used. A significator is a card that represents something else. Perhaps a person; then the Man or Woman card is used. In some readings, the significator is chosen and cards are dealt around it. In others, such as a Grand Tableau, it falls where it may, and then cards around it show how they may affect it. A significator may also represent money (Fish card), family (House card), or friends (Dog card). These are only examples.

GLOSSARY OF SYNONYMS

For each card symbol, we will explore not just what the meaning is, but where it comes from, which may be summed up in two sentences.

What is it?

What does it do?

Also, it is important to remember that interpretations for Lenormand cards are quite different from Tarot cards. The meaning of the Moon in Lenormand is vastly different from the Moon in Tarot.

As we discuss each card, some cards engender many words. Other cards, few.

Reading Lenormand is simply developing a relationship with the art that displays the symbol.

You will note that the card titles are in Spanish. This also will add yet another layer to "What is it?" and "What does it do?"

EL JINETE 1

RIDER

Imagine it's the mid-1800s. A rider comes down the road. You greet them. They dismount and walk their horse a bit. They chat and give news from up the road, what they have seen. The Rider represents a visit that brings new information (which is different than card 13: Child). It is not Machiavellian (the information may be good or bad—but not the intent in which it is provided). It is not a formal email, which falls under "letter." It may also be a bit of a "Paul Revere" type of ride.

Casual conversion, text message, messenger, delivery, carrier, mule, news.

EL TRÉBOL 2

CLOVER

When picked, they begin to wilt, so Clover is a little luck, or a short window of opportunity that may be closing—act quickly (do not get your fingers caught). If you do not play, you cannot win. Where there is no risk, there is no reward. Folks press clover in books to hide the "opportunity not taken." Clover always reminds us to lean toward "risk assumption" rather than "risk aversion."

Small luck, opportunity, unexpected, optimistic; lessens impact of neighboring negative cards.

EL BARCO 3

SHIP

The principle of this card is movement. Usually seen as a "travel" card, it also stands for wishes, as well as commerce. It is not simply journeys, but the resources invested into travel and trade over distances.

Travel, and wishes, aspirations, desires, opportunities, journey, adventure, distance. The moving of goods and persons. Border crossings. Also, journeys by ship took a long time. So, this can also indicate a long period of time. "Waiting for your ship to come in" is a good metaphor for desires and aspirations that are unfulfilled, as indicated by this card.

A good, positive card.

LA CASA 4

HOUSE

The house is where you live. It represents your secure space (regardless if it's owned or rented). It represents stability and family. A sign of success.

Casa, abode, where you live, your personal space, private life, private affairs, and "what one does behind closed doors."

EL ÁRBOL 5

TREE

A curious card generally interpreted as health. In a Grand Tableau, it is the card concerning health (the closer to the significator, the more important and concerning the health message). It also stands for "deep-rooted" things. What grows well grows slow. But if the roots are too close to the house, it is not good.

Growth, deep rooted, immobile.

LAS NUBES 6

CLOUDS

Clouds block our vision. May signify confusion, complications, and uncertainty.

No vista, obscured, unable to speak (or express one's self), confusion. Storminess, sometimes even frightening and violent. Things to the right are obscured; to the left, revealed (but if it's on the left, it is in danger). Clouds move.

La Serpiente

LA SERPIENTE 7

SNAKE

Snakes represent danger, so it is easy to view the situation as dire. La Serpiente may also represent wiring, plumbing, or the intestinal tract (twisting, and complicated). It may mean "unnecessarily complicated." It may represent a rival in love. Someone close.

An enemy, betrayal, complications, deceit, detour, seduction.

EL ATAÚD 8

COFFIN

Too many see El Ataúd and think "Death." Here, it simply means endings. Some endings are good (paying off a loan). Some things should be buried. Also, it is important to remember that life expectancies are quite different now than they were in 1799 (when Das Spiel der Hofnung was first published).

Not transformation. What goes into a coffin does not transform. It decomposes. It is gone and buried, or it sits in a box on the shelf.

El Ramo 9

EL RAMO 9

BOUQUET

Flowers are colorful, aromatic; a multilayered gift. We may have lost the language of bouquets as used during the 18th and 19th centuries. The choosing of the individual flowers carried entire messages for the recipient.

Gift, good luck, improvement of situation, assistance.

LA MACHETE 10

MACHETE

Traditionally, the Scythe.

It cuts. That is it. A machete cuts. It is a tool of work. A dull machete makes hard work even more difficult.

Risk, aggression, accident, criminality, cutting, sharp, surgeries, toil. Deadlines. Skimming (cutting) off the top.

El Látigo 11

EL LÁTIGO 11

WHIP

A whip is a tool used to strike animals or people to exert control, guidance, or compliance through pain or fear of pain.

Disagreements, arguments, anger, irritation, discord, and discipline. It usually begins with words and results in situations requiring some "cleanup" (*la escoba*).

LOS BÚHOS 12

OWLS

Owls (and birds in general) transmit information via hoots, hisses, songs, and chirps. To humans, they (birds especially) appear nervous. In the Pacific Northwest, owls hoot when it is going to rain, telling their "friends" that they should eat now, since prey will run for cover in the rain; thus, warnings.

Orally related information (mouth to ear). Phone calls. Communication. Nervousness.

EL NIÑO 13

CHILD

This is a new thing, or person. Something "in progress" or in its infancy. Also, entertainments (fun producing) and games.

Nueva. New thing. Newly met person. An existing child or grandchild. Childlike. Games. Child can represent a question of honesty or truth, and Child itself may indicate some factor that is misunderstood, or a conclusion drawn from ignorance of all facts (think games): "Is she pregnant?" "She's 70, no." Naivety will eat away at money.

EL ZORRO 14

FOX

Zorro appears sneaky because they do their homework. They learn the lay of the land, look for escape routes. It is not personal; it is what they do. So, this includes spying or wiretaps. It also represents the self-employed, since they must be clever and flexible in business. Whereas La Serpiente represents a danger from someone known, El Zorro is a danger from unknown sources.

Wrongness, deception, deceit, a crafty person. Context is important here, and one needs to note the surrounding negative or positive cards.

EL OSO 15

BEAR

Bears are powerful and protective (of their cubs and resources).

Mother-in-law or boss, person in authority, protect what is theirs, what they have built. Large, overweight, hairy, resources, courage, and strength. Could represent a large income.

STARS

Stars have been used by sailors and travelers for years as a means of navigation.

Focus, purpose, hopes and dreams, the "why" of long-term goals. If you have focus, you may create your own luck—and "She" will assist.

LA GARZA 17

STORK

When the going gets tough, storks leave. Storks follow food and tend to be seasonal, returning to where they were comfortable and found resources. A sign of good luck. When storks leave, it serves as an early warning system; when they are not comfortable, something is wrong.

Changing (usually for the better), moving, patterns.

EL PERRO 18

DOG

Although this card is the card representing your best friend, there are circumstances (see surrounding cards) where we are reminded that dogs may chew shoes or ruin the leather couch. Not that they intend to, but it is in their nature to chew, and well, it smells like you and you have been gone too long. Context and neighboring cards are important.

Loyal person, usually one's best friend, partner, companion, usually trustworthy, a third person. That said, dogs can attack and bite; they guard and thus are wary of strangers and unknown situations, often barking, snarling, even attacking.

La Torre 19

LA TORRE 19

TOWER

A watchtower historically allows us to see things far off, sometimes as a lookout for danger. Or it may ring a bell to alert us. So, we derive our main interpretation from those who may build towers: governments, religious institutions, and large corporations. Towers stand for a long time and thus imply longevity.

Government, authorities, libraries, school. Isolation (prison), being alone.

EL JARDÍN 20

GARDEN

There was a time when public gardens were popular gathering spots, the predecessor of today's shopping malls. They'd have bandstands and picnics; people would go to parks to see, be seen, and meet friends and relatives, and to make new acquaintances.

Your network, public, or social club or fraternity; safe harbor, social rules, witnesses, public places, the public, meeting, party, social gatherings.

LA MONTAÑA 21

MOUNTAIN

Bandidos viven en las montañas. Most often seen as a force outside our control, a sudden obstacle. "The Enemy." The mountain is never personal (like the Snake card). However, we must remain open to the fact that we may be our own enemy. This card implies motion (doing) and getting stopped. To continue will require much planning.

Obstacles and delays, a blockage, remote. A long time. May also serve as a blocker, or a shield between two cards.

EL CRUCE 22

CROSSROADS

Implies movement. Crossroads are historically magical places. They are where decisions are made. Sometimes good . . .

Decisions, choices, options; failure to decide stops movement and is a decision in itself.

LOS RATONES 23

MICE

Mice. What can we say? They are never good.

Loss, theft, sometimes illness. An "eating away at" someone or something (even time).

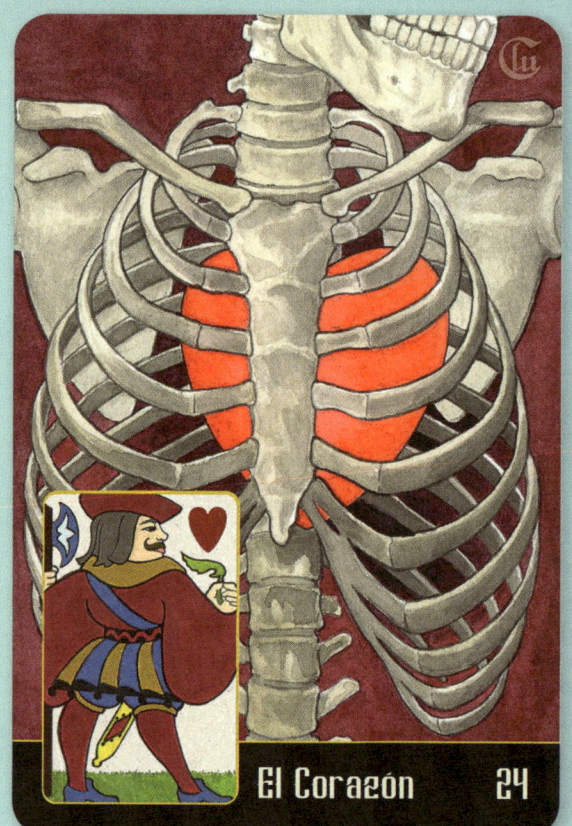

HEART

The card of love.
    Joy, love, emotions, good fortune, reconciliation, charity, solidarity.

EL ANILLO 25

RING

Many see this card as "marriage." However, it is so much more. It is more about commitments, cooperation, and, most importantly, cycles.

Contracts, things of a cyclical nature, monthly, yearly. Recurring obligations. It can indicate marriage, personal or business. It is a connection between two entities.

BOOK

A book holds information and knowledge and may represent the study to gain what is hidden inside.

Information, data, written documents. Education, academia, study. Many readers include secret information or data, depending on which side of the book is "open" to the significator (information is hidden or known).

LA CARTA 27

LETTER

Letter writing used to be common. Here, it represents a formal communication, as opposed to Rider or Owls.

Formal communication. Email or postal. Documentation, résumé, permits; can even be a newspaper, or a will. Generally, it is good news.

CABALLERO 28

MAN

The man in the reading (if the reading is for a man, this represents him).

Also, the primary man in the life of a woman if the reading is for a woman. Masculine qualities of a situation. Alternately, if the primary man is in a relationship with another man, the second man card would be added to the deck. The Woman card may or may not be excluded.

CABALLERO 28

MAN

The man in the reading (if the reading is for a man, this represents him).

Also, the primary man in the life of a woman if the reading is for a woman. Masculine qualities of a situation. Alternately, if the primary man is in a relationship with another man, the second man card would be added to the deck. The Woman card may or may not be excluded.

SEÑORA 29

WOMAN

The woman in the reading (if the reading is for a woman, this represents her).

Also, the primary woman in the life of a man if the reading is for a man. Feminine qualities of a situation. Alternately, if the primary woman is in a relationship with another woman, the second woman card would be added to the deck. The Man card may or may not be excluded.

SEÑORA 29

WOMAN

The woman in the reading (if the reading is for a woman, this represents her).

Also, the primary woman in the life of a man if the reading is for a man. Feminine qualities of a situation. Alternately, if the primary woman is in a relationship with another woman, the second woman card would be added to the deck. The Man card may or may not be excluded.

LOS LIRIOS 30

LILIES

Lilies is an interesting card. Flowers are the sex organs for plants. The lily is used both in weddings and funerals. It is a card that focuses on the senses and our enjoyment of those senses. In many societies, this pleasure of our senses is eschewed, so lily may have some negative cultural connotations.

Sex, pleasure, devotion, sexuality; virtue, purity, and morality; humility, wisdom, and winter. I have seen this referred to as "a catchall card in German tradition."

EL SOL 31

SUN

What does the Sun do? It gives warmth and light, allows things to grow. Shines a light on difficult situations so they may be resolved, and truth can be revealed. The Sun is seen as masculine.

Warmth, goodness, open, daytime, vistas (you can see where you are going). Success, victory, power, and truth.

LA LUNA 32

MOON

What does the Moon do? It reflects sunlight. It is about reflection of how others see you, your reputation (usually concerning your work). The Moon is seen as feminine.

Your reputation, how others see you; may be related to artistic talent, fame, and recognition.

La Llave 33

LA LLAVE 33

KEY

The "Yes" card of the deck. That said, there may be times where it represents a "locking" as opposed to "unlocking" (rare).

Solutions, success, deliverance, new undertakings, meant to be.

LOS PECES 34

FISH

Although seen and used as the financial or economic significator, it both does and does not mean money. It is more about abundance. Ever try to hold a fish? Holding money is not dissimilar.

Abundance (money or things), finance, money, business, free movement, gain, and understanding values. Also, Fish may indicate drinking, or water.

El Ancla 35

EL ANCLA 35

ANCHOR

Anchors in Lenormand decks are usually shown on dry land—where they are worthless and serve as useless lawn ornaments. Anchors work when they are submerged, unseen, underwater, holding their vessel safe.

Representing stability and security, the anchor keeps one in a safe place. Its association with steadfastness leads us to equate it with our employment. Unable to move, "hard and fast" has its own problems.

LA CRUZ 36

CROSS

What is a cross? To some it is seen as a sign of faith. But it got that meaning from its being an object of torture (and you must carry your own—by yourself) and death.

Pain, grief, a burden, misery, harsh troubles, duty, conviction, and convicted. A "cross to bear." Not a happy card.

SYMBOLS, SUITS, AND CLUSTERS

Various card symbol meanings fall into varied groups or clusters.

The Danger Cluster: The Serpent, Mice, Mountain, Fox, and Machete fall into the category.

What is of note, is that this cluster contains four Clubs suits, and one Diamond. When we equate this to the original German suit meanings, we find 4 Acorns (bitter) most of the 'bad' cards fall into the Clubs (acorn) suit. The exception is Machete which is a Diamond (in the original German suit—a bell. Bells are warnings, alarms, things we need to pay attention to).

The Danger cluster contains cards that rarely have good characteristics. The word Danger should not be taken as a threat to life, but a cause for upsets, and delays.

The Mountain is not a person. It's immovable. You can't move it.

The Serpent is a person you know and should be wary of (but also complications).

The Fox is a third person you probably do not know. And here we must be careful because it's not always a danger (think the self-employed trying to keep up with the times doing their homework – or are they spying? Note surrounding cards).

Mice steal. It's their nature. If near a Career card, assets are in danger.

The Love Cluster: The Heart, Ring, and Anchor. The Heart is the most important card to look for in questions of relationship, and the steadfastness of the Anchor.

The Ring is tricky. If to the left of the significator, the ongoing cycle of commitment may be lessening. To the right of the significator the cycle of commitment may be beginning.

The Ring is a Club, as it often represents things outside of a relationship (contracts & commitments) which can be a worry.

Anchor is a Spade, for it represents the steadfastness of commitment.

The Heart is the usual symbol for love. And its suit is Hearts.

The Career Cluster: The Ship, Anchor, Fish represent abundance, career, and resources.

We wait for our ship to come in. Ship is in the Spades suit, the suit of growth. The Anchor is also in the suit of Spades and represents steadiness of assets.

One wants Fish to fall near other benevolent cards. Fish falling amongst the suit of Diamonds indicates assets should not be ignored or taken for granted.

When coffin or Danger cards are tucked up against your Career cards, take note.

Circle of Trust: The Child, Dog, Garden. These are the cards that may negate the difficult cards in a spread, when near to the significator.

How many more clusters can you find?

THE MINI-TABLEAUS

THE 3×3 SPREAD
Also known as the nine-card box

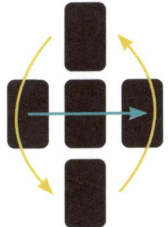 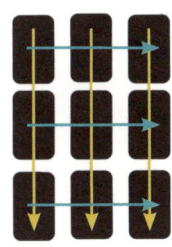

This spread is versatile and, once learned, can answer almost any question with exquisite detail. The description sounds complicated, until you do it a couple of times. It is easy and useful.

You begin by laying out three rows of three cards. Alternately, some may choose to use a significator as the central card, laying the other eight cards around it. I have found that to be unnecessary, but I do encourage you to play with both methods and choose the one you find most useful.

You may read this as a simple past-present-future spread, but there is so much more when we begin to expand our vision and find things a past-present-future spread would miss.

We are going to move around the box, using the eight three-card spreads and the two four-card spreads that the Mini-Tableau provides for us.

The center card is your focus card. The main focus in the answer to the question.

The four corners provide a quick overview. It is similar to a blurb on the back cover of a paperback book. It gives hints about the plot but does not examine the details and twists of the plot.

The first column may be read as a three-card spread of the past, the second column may be read as a three-card spread of the present, and the right-hand column may be read as a future. There are also readers who ignore the past-present-future and simply use the columns as three sentences that provide longer descriptions to the overall "story." The bottom cards of each column are weighed down by what is above them. They're heavier and more difficult to manage.

The top row, I interpret as things that are "up in the air," out of our control. Some refer to it as a thought line, or the worry line. The center row is our most likely outcome if we do absolutely nothing, and the bottom row represents things we are able to control and something we can act on.

The center cards of the top row, the right-hand column, the bottom row, and the left-hand column form a diamond. Various names have been ascribed by people who use this. The diamond contains the cards closest to the focus card. So, by the time you get to the diamond, a lot has been revealed. The diamond is one more layer of issues that are close to the focus.

The three-card diagonal from the upper right to the lower left is a line of defense. Things to contemplate to prevent misfortune.

The diagonal from the upper left to the lower right is your line of power or authority. Things to bring into action to exert your own influence on a situation.

The lower left card in this Mini-Tableau is often referred to as the Exit card. It is the last and final word of the spread. If it is a negative card, you will want to review the spread to find if there are things to mitigate a poor outcome.

The top left-hand card is sometimes referred to as the "trigger-card" (some call it the Fate card). It is "out of control" and presses down like a weight on everything below it. The most important aspect of this card is not how to change it, but how one is going to respond to it.

LA PEQUEÑA CRUZ
The Little Cross

This is a lovely spread that works for those difficult questions such as "Is he coming back?" or "Are they going away?"

You lay out the three cards in a row. The next card goes above the center card, and another below.

Now we imagine the top cards on a clock face. The top card is at 12, and we move clockwise, numbering the cards 3, 6, and 9.

We can at this point do two three-card-spread readings. We can read the row, and the column. We can mirror the two sides and the top and bottom.

But here is the really beautiful part of the La Pequeña Cruz.

Imagine the sitter to be at the 6 (you can even place a significator here). What is at three o'clock is moving toward the sitter. This could mean that romance, assets, work, emotions, or whatever is moving toward the sitter. You may want to include both the 12 and 3 as moving toward the sitter. It may show that their situation is gaining in size or force. It may show that "they" are coming to visit.

The card at nine o'clock (followed by twelve o'clock) shows what is moving away from the sitter.

These may also show changes in the sitter's emotional life, how they "feel about something," moving toward or moving away.

It may show money being paid out, or that the matter in question is moving away (leaving), or that the sitter is going to "visit" them (moving away).

So, 6 represents "us," and the here and now.

The 9 is losing importance, movement away.

The 3 signifies what is coming to us or gaining importance.

COLOR, ARTE Y SEÑORA DE LA NOCHE

There are seven colors of La Santa Muerte. You'll notice different candle colors used by devotees. The colors they use are important.

Blue is for education, comprehension, concentration, and insight.

Red is for love and passion.

Green is for law, justice, legal matters, land, and fertility.

White is neutral and brings peace, harmony, and protection and helps keep us on the true path.

Black is for protection or harm (or both). It is the most potent energy to work with. Use caution; more than fingers can get burned.

Gold is for abundance, prosperity, and material success.

Purple enhances healing both in physical

and mental realms.

Those are the primary seven colors. There is one more additional color that sometimes shows up.

Brown is used in matters when dealing with the dead.

Choose your candles wisely.

In the creation process of *La Santa Muerte Lenormand* deck, the artist Callie L. French and I discussed each card in detail. We'd both reject sketches, with some cards taking many attempts. Phone calls were made. Voices were raised. Each card's image is the result of hours of research, contemplation, and discussion from many angles. Hair was pulled.

And then we'd get to the colors to be used. And the waters got calm. We would feel at peace. Each color for each card was also carefully discussed and chosen. Every card—shades, hue, tone, density.

You may at first disagree with the result. But trust in the results of working with the art. For therein lies the ultimate secret.

I give thanks to Callie L. French, who takes visions and manifests them as art. I thank Dr. Elizabeth Claassen for telepathy.

La paz sea contigo y tu familia.

—**Dan M. Pelletier**, January 25, 2021

REFERENCES

Chesnut, R. Andrew. *Devoted to Death: Santa Muerte, the Skeleton Saint*. Oxford: Oxford University Press, 2012.

Prower, Tomás. *La Santa Muerte: Unearthing the Magic and Mysticism of Death*. Minneapolis: Llewellyn, 2015.

Rollin, Tracey. *Santa Muerte: The History, Rituals, and Magic of Our Lady of the Holy Death*. Newburyport, MA: Weiser Books, 2017.